Written and illustrated by Kiran Badola. All rights reserved © 2017

Camelia with a hump so defined,
flaunted it with finesse never confined.

To be seen was a mighty hippo,
meandering along she said, "Hello!"

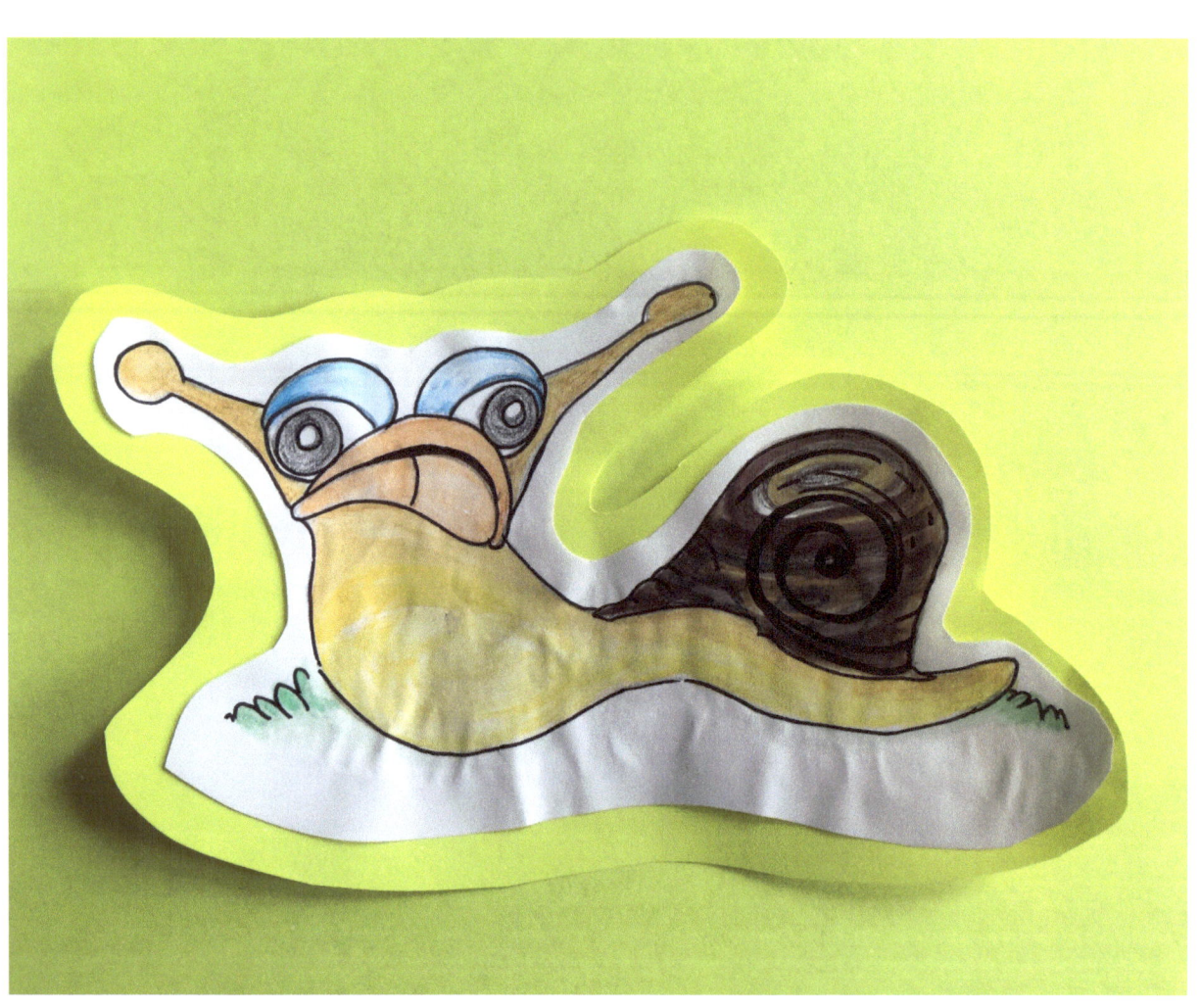

A snail caught all that occurred,
to have a fantastic time he conquered.

Far in the distance oblivious to all,
stood a majestic tortoise after a crawl.

Along came a flamingo mesmerizing,
Camelia seized the moment imbibing.

A frog sat prudent a butterfly fluttering,
Camelia drew them to their inkling.

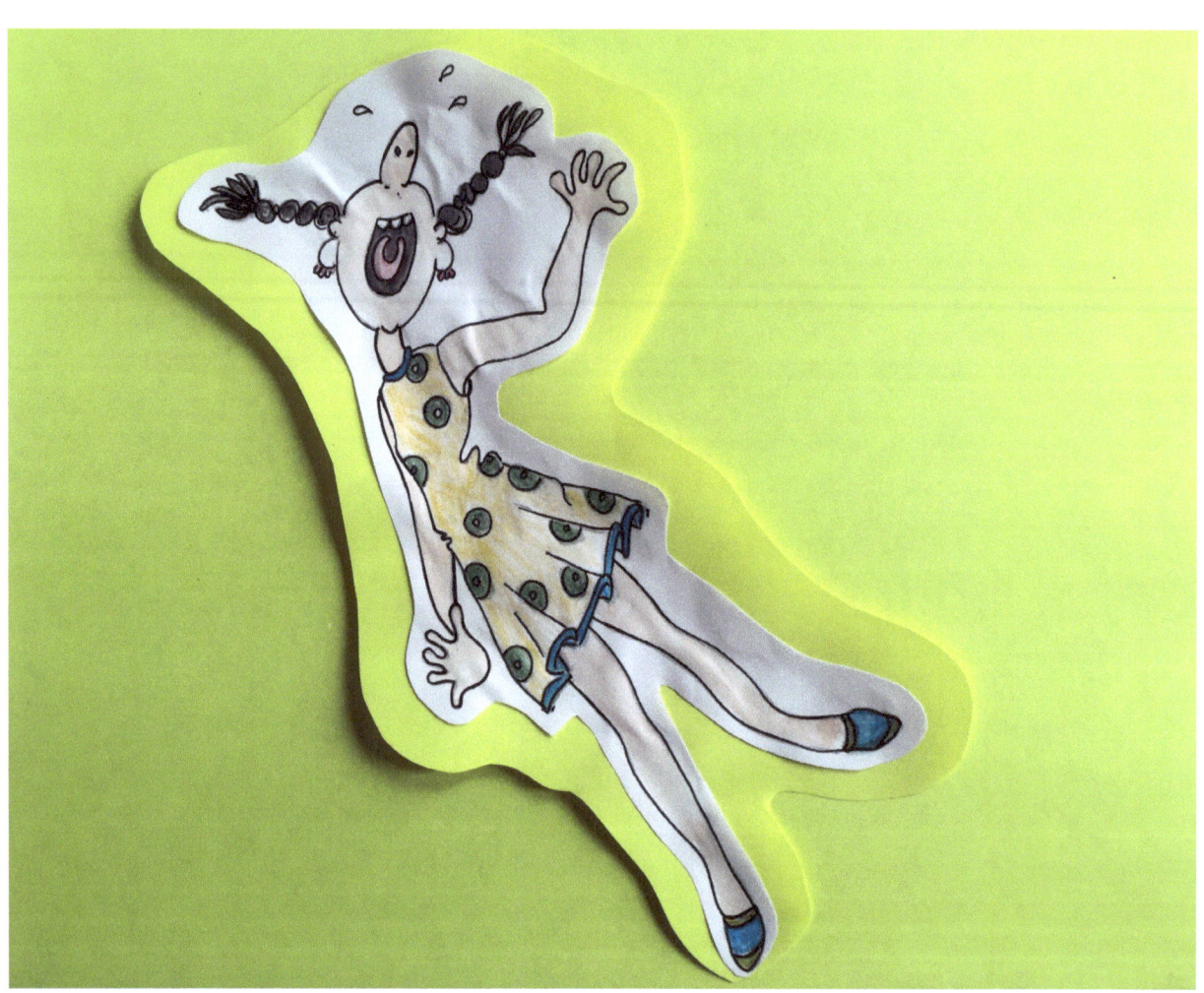

Living life oh so splendid,
a girl pranced joyously unended.

An owl hooted as a viper slithered near,
off plodded Camelia obscuring fear.

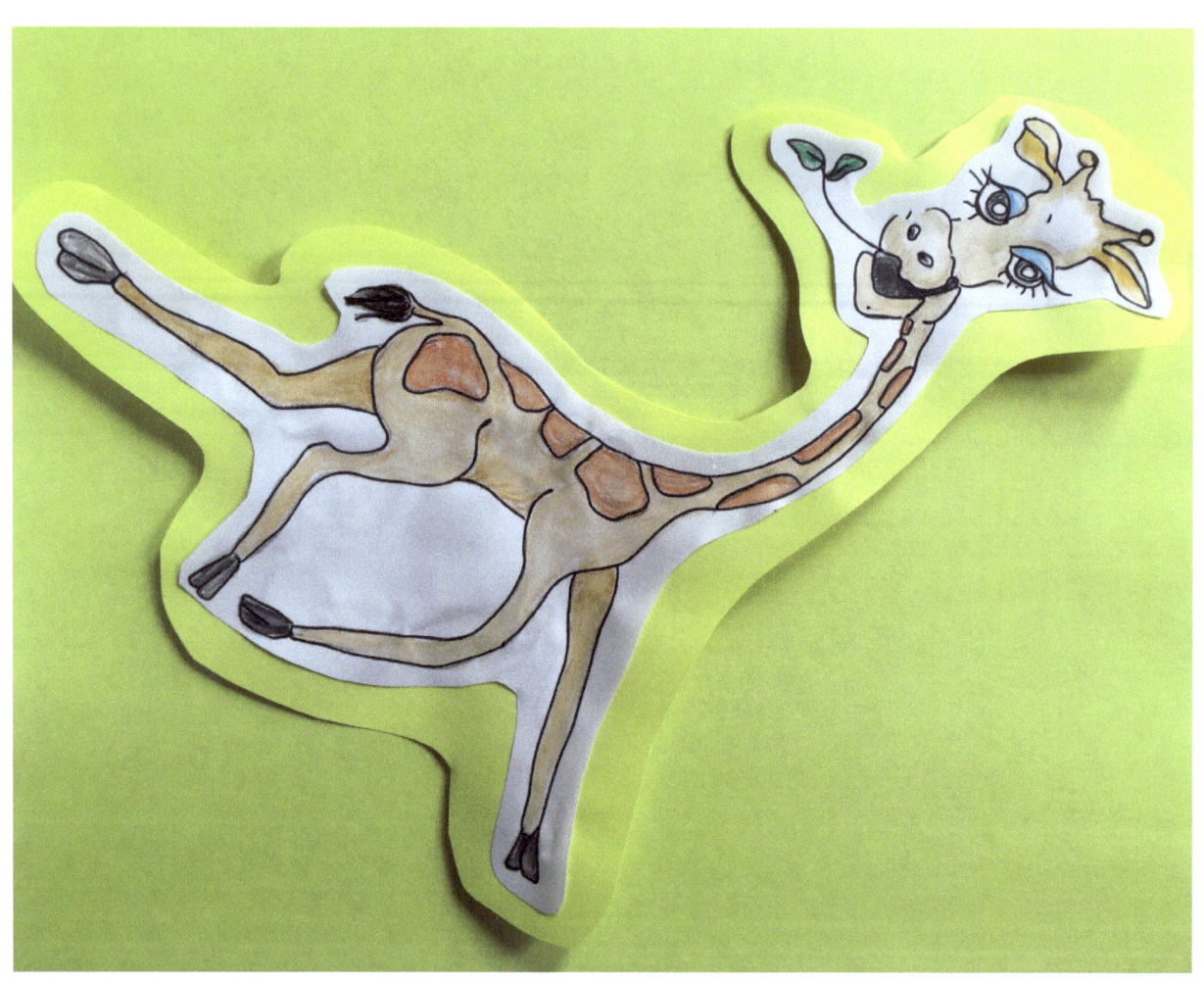

The pleasantly festooned existence,
made it a place to live in an instance.

VOCABULARY

Flaunted - Show off

Finesse - Cleverness

Confined - Uncomfortable

Defined - Clear

Mighty -   Powerful

Meandering -   Turning

Mesmerizing -   Attractive

Seized -   Grab

Imbibing -   Consuming

Oblivious -   Unaware

Majestic -   Impressive

Conquered -   Win

Prudent -   Wise

Fluttering -   Flapping

Fantastic -   Excellent

Inkling -   Understanding

Splendid -   Beautiful

Pranced -   Jumped

Slithered -   Slid

Plodded -   Walk heavily

Obscuring -   Masking

Festooned -   Decorated

Instance -   Bit